Dedication

To the bits and pieces of our lives, Stashed away in the memories we've held so dear to -

You will never be forgotten.

_Kai

Table Of Contents

Chapters:

Introduction

Life is filled of memories;
Too pure to be left in the shadows,
Too breath-taking to be buried in cemeteries,
Too worthy to be lost to the universe.
This is the **remnant** of all our lives,
Captured and frozen in time:
The best and worst of all of us.
It is raw, wholesome and true.

Birth

"Behold I make all things new."

The Moment

Placed her blood, sweat, and tears,
Into a minuscule jar.
Watching as the stick turned blue;
Waiting, it grew.
Water spilt on the floor –
Soon to embrace.

Ripping in half,
Left for dead,
The agony she beheld.

Spectacle of attraction.
Perpetuated screams,
Gripping fingers.
Monitors beep –
The empty spaces between.

Oxygen present:
They both breathe.
Sigh of relief –
Life is a two way street.

Mama Loves You Baby

(To mama's pride and joy.)

Mama loves you baby.
Mama cradles you –
With proud hands.
Ray of sunshine,
Penetrating,
The mornings and afternoons.
Anything you want, it's yours.
Precious cherry blossoms.
Fruit of her womb.
Mama worked hard for you.
Never leave your side,
She will pray.
Watch with care:
She will guard.
The promised land –
A bright future.
She will go to hell and back for you.

Mama loves you baby.
Mama counts the days,
Until you are grown.
Always you are,
her little one.
She will lock your tiny hands,
In hers,
Even though they are fully sized.
Into your eyes,

She will see her smile.
Shed a tear,
For her heart cries –
One day you will spread your wings and fly.
To the one she has overwhelmingly loved,
How could she ever dare to let you go?

Mama loves you baby,
And forever,
You will be her cherished child.

Pint Size

Swaddled fingers interlock.
Kisses, Wet – Leaves a mark.
Reminds,
Of the love shared.
Coo's and Ouu's of wonder.
Eyes astonishing,
Likc shooting stars.

Counting sheep,
Refusing sleep,
So much out there to learn.
Stay little,
This way, for long.
Embraced in mommy's arms.
Safely
–Away from harm.

Terrible Twos

Terrible Twos,
Burst your fuse, Pops
– no replacement.
Unable to find their shoes,
Most when they are needed.
Climbing walls,
Like Spiderman,
Call this their enjoyment.
Tumbling to and fro,
Apparently, no feelings.
Laughing out mischievously.
The ways of a child.
Full of Grace, Full of smiles,
In the end – they are mines.
Glad to call them ours,
Truly love divine.

My Daddy

"I will not give up!
Cause my daddy?
My daddy's always winning!
My daddy's always winning everything for me!"

— Ameila, 4.

Princess

Princesses sparkle,
In glamorous gowns.
Swirling heels,
That never scuffs the ground.

Soldiers guarding your every move,
Maidens to care for your every cry,
You alone are the king's special prize.

He will buy for you,
Both diamonds and pearls.
Kiss the fore of your precious hand.
Take you to ballrooms,
Waltz you in circles,
Before any prince ever can.

Banquet tables of desirable cuisines.
Croquet embellished about the wrist.
You alone are the king's special prize!

In this story of ole –

The princess is you.
Daddy is the king.
He will be there for you in everything.

Pitter Patter

Crawl to mama, Little one,
I am here.
Arms stretched before –
There is a way.
Take pitter patter, flat,
Across the floor.
It is clean,
Mommy ensured.
She sees your smile,
Arise!
she cheers you on,
"You can do this!"
Encourage and bless,
Their little hearts.
Dribbles,
At the corner lip.
Mini push ups.
"There you go!"
The love,
How much can one endure?
Cute, you are, mi amor.
Crawl to mama, Little one.
There is much left for you in store.

Daughter

Thank You for choosing me.
Thank you for giving me the opportunity.
Thank you for seeing me as worthy.
I promise to always be there.
I promise to go the extra mile.
I promise to make you smile.
You are a precious little girl.
You are lovely from the core.
You are designed like no other.
God made us,
Mother and daughter.
You are everything I ever hoped for.
I only hope,
I am all you ever hoped for too.

Sonshine

You are my sonshine,
My only sonshine.
You make me happy,
When skies are gray.

Your glistening eyes,
IIow thcy hypnotize.
Squealing laughs,
Like ringing of bells.
Your hugs – suffocate,
Yet, I don't mind.
How plain of a life,
Without my son held tight.
There is nothing in this world,
That I would cherish more.

You'll never know, son,
How much I love you,
Please don't take my sonshine away.

Blessing

Blessing of God,
You've changed my world,
I am glad that you are here.

Adolescence

"The signs of the time."

Teen Girls

(To the rollercoaster of adolescence.)

It all starts at age thirteen,
That moment you convert from a child,
Into a teen.
A girl who has now become a teenager,
It is the beginning of many stories.
And by the time we hit age twenty,
We have a book load of interesting stories.
Some interesting stories we'd have to tell,
Some interesting stories indeed.

Let's begin by clearing the air;
Let's talk on a topic we never want to share,
Let's talk about when we had our first cramp –
When we started our period,
With the tears we shed here and there.

We had now become an epicenter of raging hormones,
Progesterone and Oestrogen,
Running down to our core –
To our brain more and more.
Desires they start to roar,
And boys didn't seem so icky anymore.

Your first crush,
The first guy that has ever made you day dream.
Of him,
You could not get enough.

To say "hi,"
It seemed like way too much.
And when he'd flash that smile,
Look at you from the corner of his eyes –
All you could do is blush.

At age sixteen,
We know our life isn't always plush,
A Lot of the time we react in a rush.
It isn't always perfect;
We have our flaws,
We have our secrets –
I'm just giving 'girl talk'.
There are those days,
We're supposed to go home after school,
Yet, we chill a little longer with the girls –
We know the boys will be arriving soon.
We walk the long way around;
Because nothing seemed cooler,
Than walking in the afternoon,
With such an amazing dude –
His arms wrapped around you.

He stops in his place,
And you stop too.
He looks into your eyes,
Then your lips:
You're mesmerized.

Is this the moment you've been waiting for?
Is this the moment you've anticipated?
He's getting closer to you,

He kisses you.
At age eighteen.
You've been through at least one break-up,
You tried making up,
You've even tried on different make up.
You scream,
"It's for girl power!"
But in truth,
You don't think you're pretty enough.
You've used a lot of concealer,
And still you can't conceal your mental breakdown,
You're tired –
You just want a shoulder to lean on.

It's not you alone,
Other girls are on the same path as you,
All worn out,
Tired of life punches,
And tired of guys too.
You try dating girls,
Cause, hey,
Girls understand girls,
And what have I to lose?

You feel emotionally attached.
You say you love her and you love her really bad.
You've even kissed her a few times –
Not the cheek to cheek kind.
You've taken showers together,
Seen her most intimate parts.
You feel like you've known her forever,
That this can actually last,

But then it doesn't.
It was merely temporary bliss that wore off after a while.

You're nineteen,
And you realize,
It's just one more year before you're no longer considered a teen,
Instead,
A young adult.

You're caught up in the parties,
The drinking,
The sex.
Your mother warned you;
Scorned you,
She told you,
Stay away,
Those things will leave you in a mess.

You're in such a wreck,
That You don't realize, there isn't much of you left.

Another guy came into the picture–
You met him through one of your girlfriends.
He told you how you're special,
You're different,
That he likes that.
He told you how your body is number one;
That he had options,
but for you,
He'd drop them.

He lied though.

He never did.
He texted them –
Met up with them on weekends.
You really weren't in for the drama,
So:
You left him.

You're twenty, single,
You have a few drinks now and then.
You still haven't figured out life as yet.
You keep close to the friends you have –
The true ones,
The fake ones,
To you,
Are dead .

You listen to your music on low,
There is a sign on your door that says,
"Do Not Disturb."
You think back to a long time ago,
Where did those happy memories go?

God forbid you die young,
I only hope, for you,
Long life to come.
And so be it,
There are many more stories to be written,
Here after,
There are many more stories to come.

It all starts at age thirteen,
That moment you convert from a child,

Into a teen.
A girl who has now become a teenager,
It is the beginning of many stories.
And by the time we hit age twenty,
We have a book load of interesting stories.
Some interesting stories we'd have to tell,
Some interesting stories indeed.

Blue

No one noticed the girl in blue.
No one noticed how she strategically chose her seating
arrangement in the corner of the room,
Every time.
No one noticed how she gazed her wondering eyes across the
room,
Hoping at least one person will say, "Hi".
No one saw the dying look in her eyes as she realized people
were just passing her by.
No one noticed how her facial expression ceased to be anything
other than alive.

No one noticed –
Or no one cared.

No one noticed the girl with her head face down on the table.
No one noticed, even though she sat in the front of the classroom
making her presence that much more known.
No one noticed that if they would've taken a few minutes to ask
if she's okay, that they would've more than made her day.

The teacher showed up to class,
Told everyone to stand –
And there,
Her eyes filled of tears,
Enough to fill a glass.
And yet –
No one noticed –

Or no one cared.

No one noticed the girl sitting amongst the crowd.
No one noticed that she couldn't smile.
No one knew, she was about to blow,
That she couldn't take it anymore,
So she stormed out the door.
No one realized she was trying to keep her cool.
No one noticed, she was hurting and didn't know what to do.
No one noticed she was going through a rough patch,
And on top of that, she felt like an outcast.

No one noticed –
Or no one cared.

No one noticed the lonely girl in the room.
No one noticed the lonely girl in the room.
No one noticed the lonely girl in the room,
Because no one noticed the girl in blue.

Lonely

She always walked the streets alone.
She knew how to cover her bruises, so they wouldn't show.
She was everything except bold.
She was the one hurting,
The girl in the sad story.
"Why?"
She'd question she was born.
Was she a girl or boy,
Truly unsure.
Loud music was an escape for her soul.
Behind closed doors,
Her tears unfold.
And for the most anything go'd.
For most of her life,
Her lips were closed.
Hoodies kept her warm,
While life made her heart cold.
Always she knew –
All she knew,
Was a life, set aside,
And her existence never catered to.

A message to mothers

Dear Mom,
We are sorry for not washing the dishes;
For not cleaning our rooms,
For stressing you out,
Giving you gray hair,
Making you look older than you need to.

We sincerely apologize.
We can't promise you that we'll be the best,
But we will try.
Hopefully, one day,
We'll make you proud.
Address all the shortcomings that made you frown.

Our behavior, we know, makes us seem as if we don't care.
How we effortlessly ignore you –
Then you nag about it,
And nag about it.
And continue and continue to nag about it,
But rest assure,
We do hear you.

We do see you and notice –
In the mornings, when you're up,
shuffled around the house.
Shower running; clothes out ironed, windows opened, radio on,
breakfast cooking.

While 10 o' clock is around the corner and we're still laying in bed.
How you multitask like that is a wonder.
Yet, everyday without fail, you keep at it;
You keep moving, keep giving, keep pushing.
Even on those days when you're fed up,
And you're certain this time,
You will move out and leave us here.

You still came home.
Mom you've never left us, and that to us means the world.
So please, forgive us, when all we do is fail: Your hard work displayed in vain.
We know life without you wouldn't be the same.

Though we hardly say it; Mom, we appreciate you, we love you,
Thanks for everything,

Sincerely,
Your loving heart strings.

I Don't Know

(Teen Pregnancy.)

I don't know what to do,
I think I've bitten off more than I can chew,
Frustrated by the things I no longer control.

What if there is no going back from here?
What if forever my life has changed?
No longer am I the same.

I wish that day had never happened.

That I couldn't make it, That things came up.
I was so disoriented, That wasn't me.
I didn't see myself in the mirror in front of me.

What will I say, How can I say it?

Consumed by fear,
This is too much for me.
Hoping things will get better,
I am utterly afraid.

Please, I don't know what to do.

Cut

Don't cut yourself short–

Don't cut the wrist that bleeds.
Don't cut the throat that breathes.
Don't cut your hopes and dreams.

Don't end it under the pretense,
where you feel less than need be.

The cuts are deep,
And the cuts do hurt.
They leave a scar,
And tears do run.

Yet, wait, hold on.
And please,
Don't cut yourself short.

Overload

Sorrows drown from the inside,
There is a well within my soul.
Roaring tides in a pint sized bottle.
The pressure is condensing–
Expectantly, it explodes.
There is nothing left.
A cracked open nozzle,
Has leaked its final drop.
Exhausted of the to and fro–
Sick of being me.

Complicated

Intrusive thoughts;
Complete self doubt,
Raging war,
Non-stop.

Friendship

" Who sticks closer than a brother? "

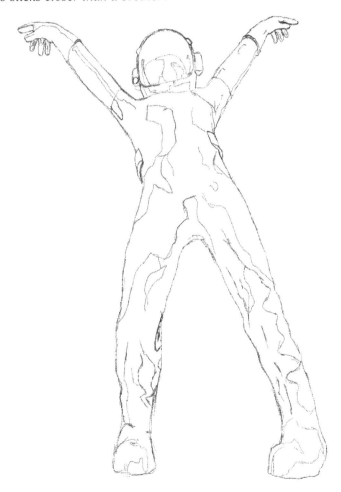

Force To be Reckoned

She was a force to be reckoned with.

The winds against the sail,
Hair behind her ear, she knew what freedom was.
Lips part, tongue out, she tasted flavors.
How she loved without eyes and always without ties –
Her beautiful fairy tale in existence.

Through the seasons she made her family proud.
On the walls,
Accomplishments came crashing down.
The facade gave way.
A rainbow distorted.
The person she became, they never wanted –
Yet, sorry never slipped her mouth.

She was picture perfect,
In a world where picture perfect isn't true.
She was that one strand of kinky hair.
Out of place, she came to embrace –
That not all forces should be reckoned with –
For the shock waves that would stir,
Not even the earth would be able to withstand it.

That Girl From Across The Room

She stood a far off just like she always did.
Never taking much notice of her surroundings,
Never to take much notice of the wandering eyes.
It didn't bother her.
She was quite different and she knew this.
She had goals.
She had dreams.
She made it her long life mission to run after,
Yet things weren't working out that way –
We all knew this.

She didn't care though.

Her dreams will always be her reality,
Unless she didn't make it.
That was her fear,
putting all this time,
Just to go to waste.

She stood a far off just like she always did.
And I watched her.
I was a wandering eye with no intentions.
I was a customer in a store just looking –
I have intentions now.
Hoping to know her –
I think she knows this.
She looks my way,
Caught in the center of my gazing eyes,

She doesn't blink and neither do I.
I want this.

The one who is unbothered –
Who has dreams that are crumbling;
And still doesn't care,

Cause she'll be damned,
If she doesn't do all she can to make them happen.
Who in my weary eyes, is beyond fearless.

She stood a far off just like she always did;
And in a beautiful, awkward, satisfying way,
Cracked me a one of a kind smile,
I'll never forget.

Friend

I know you,
I've known you,
And you know,
That I'm your friend.
Regardless of the once naysayers,
Those who seemed to see themselves as too popular to hang with us.
We've always rocked our converse.
Rock the world of those who have underestimated –
You and me,
We go way back –
Wow, we really did suck at running track.
Guys they'd come and go,
But we were never alone.
No, always we had each other and isn't that what friends are for?

True Enemy

Friends become foes,
Foes become friends.
I am convinced,
I know the true enemy.

Judas made it very clear,
We eat with the hand that bites us.

Expect the smile,
In return for a venomous kiss.

Traitors in disguise,
Dagger to the eyes,
For the man who always had his back.

Money didn't cost him a thing –
Until it cost him everything.

Exchanging built trust for dimes.
Refusing to show remorse –
Tables turned on a friend.

Hanging from a tree –
Rope lynched around the neck.

Once thicker than blood,
Now you are dead.
See, Judas taught me:
I know the true enemy.

Saving Grace

Thanks for hearing me out when no one else would.

You're my saving grace.
Here's my love, beyond measure.
An amazing sister –
Who is better off without me.

I'm a headache of confusion;
With lots of trust issues,
Still, somehow, you make the space for me.

For all the times I've failed.
Can I ever truly repay?

Thanks for hearing me out when no one else would.

Safely

I didn't want to bother you.
I wondered if you were in trouble.
That is,
Until I convinced myself,
"The less you know, the less you care."

Love

" Let him kiss me with the kisses of his mouth; for thy love is better than wine. "

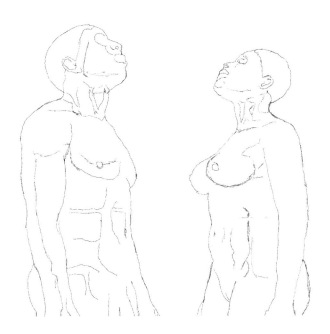

You are

You are a drop of sunlight.
Small in quantity,
Yet,
Holds the ability to shine bright.

You are radiant.
From the moment you wake in the morning,
Rubbing the sleep out of your eyes –
You show forth life.

You are a diamond.
A structure of complex carbon bonds,
holding tight.
Compressed under pressure,
Oh, so precious.

You are a treasure chest.
Hidden away in darkness,
Locked and keys thrown away,
But to break the chains,
Is to see the true worth of gems within it.

You are a girl.

Regardless of the scratches and the makeshift patches.
Regardless of the story and the unread chapters.

You are a girl.

You are a beautiful girl.
Deserving of love,
You deserve to be loved,
And you shall be loved.

Behold thee the moment of a beautiful soul,
Waiting to unfold.

Then seize it,
And you will never lose it.

You will never lose it.

Your Body

I admit.
I take more glances at you than I should.

I do.
I examine you from your head to your toe.

In my mind,
I imagine things of you and I –
Behind closed doors.

I admit.

I admit, I do in my mind.
In my mind, I do, I admit.

Only because your body,
These sins I dare to commit.
Sounds of rushing waters
through my veins,
My heart, it skips a beat again.
My forehead and the palms of my hands become quite sweaty.

Though I notice you,
I hope you don't notice,
For the little things,
I find myself falling for you.

I don't neglect your inner beauty,
I embrace it all the more.

It's quite and expensive art piece,
I only hope I can afford –

Your body.

There may have been a few times that you caught me.
There were moments, we shared a few seconds eye to eye.
Simple smiles,
Blushes,
Yet, it was too easy to say good-bye.

At face value there seemed to be nothing, nothing deemed
serious between us.
Was it perhaps we were both afraid to reveal what was really on
our minds:
Fearing one of us would reject the other?

Still I anticipated the times we would meet.
I anticipated the times where I could savor a few hours with you.
We didn't have to exchange any words.
And excuse me if I sound a bit too oversexualized,
But all I needed was the presence of –

Your body.

You do not need to wear the finest of linens.
Do not need to have the backstory of a king or queen in England.
No need for you to be the richest of rich,
Or ever acquire wealth for lavish living.
No.

That is not what I have ever required of you.

Just your existence.
Your love.

Your Body.

A Forbidden Love

From the moment I laid my eyes on you,
I can't deny,
My mind stormed with romantic thoughts.

I thought about how beautiful you were,
And how God conceived thoughts
Made you into a being.

And there you were, standing right in front of me:
A dream came true.

And in that hour, that minute, that second –
Nothing compared to you.

You had a heart of Gold –
You still do.
It's just buried beneath the dirt that others have thrown at you,
But I'll gladly grab a shovel and dig through.

Let me hold your hands and tell you how much I've missed you,
Even though you hadn't left the room.

From the moment I laid my eyes on you,
I can't deny,
My mind stormed with romantic thoughts.

"Oh, how I want you. Oh, how I want you,"

The only thing is that I was too afraid to tell you.

I Want You

I try to get you off my mind –
I won't lie,
It's hard.

Sentimental moments come,
With each one,
You're the rising star.

I find myself smiling at nothing.
The thought of You keeps me blushing.

Although, this may sound ridiculous:
I get jealous sometimes,
I wonder if you're out there in another woman's arms.

I know you aren't mines,
Still, I want you in my life.

This started as a spark.
Now, for you,
I have feelings that I can't stop.

My heart melts down to nothing,
Every time I'm in your presence –
My hands get sweaty.

And while a million thoughts may run through
my mind,

In that moment,
I can't utter a sentence to you.

I know you aren't mines,
Still, I want you in my life.

The thing is;
I don't know,
If you'd want me in your life,
too.

Boy

Yes,
It is true –
That you are not a *man*.

But,
In this moment with me –
You'd wish you were.

To Find Someone

I want someone to listen.
Through the tears;
The sweaty hands,
Cracking voices,
Disturbing mind.

I want someone to stay.
To hold me close,
Treat me as a home,
Take care until we're old.

I want someone familiar.
Who is broken;
Who doesn't mind trading burdens.
Sees no wrong in combining shambles –
Of things that were,
Into something that can be.

I need someone to love me,
And someone I can love.
Someone who knows it's okay,
To lose yourself and find it all.

Enigma

You are an enigma to me.
I want to erase,
The what if's,
The maybe's,
I don't knows.
I want to know you.
In my eyes you are worth it:
You are worth all my time.
I wish I was brave,
Whispering sweetly into those ears.
They say love,
Makes you do strange things:
I believe.
Loving I have feared,
But with you I hope not to.
They say beauty is in the eyes –
The wonders I have found in you.
My looks,
They falter.
Yet, A gorgeous soul,
I offer.
Waiting on you for some day,
That one day,
We could be ours.
I've chosen you,
And I'd choose you again.
If only you'd know,
How precious you truly are.

More

I'm not the funniest of persons,

I'm not the life of the party,

But I sure can leave you wanting *more* of me.

Hold Tight

This push and pull.
This to and fro.

This give and take –
My breath away.

She is the epitome
Of your whimsical desires.

Entrapped in the web
of your lascivious dreams.

Do not let her go.

Complete

My love is never complete without You.

Heart Break

"He will wipe away every tear from their eye."

Last Time

You said,
That would be the last time.
The last time;
You'd put your hands on me,
You'd threaten me,
You'd cheat.
You backstabbing lover–
My lover,
Or my once upon a time.
I soaked in your lies,
And made your tie-dye colors my truth.
Your, "I love you's," were sweet –
Something good to eat,
But I've learned that too much sugar
can give you rotten teeth.
So before you rob me of those –
As you have robbed me of a heart,
I'm taking whatsoever of me remains –

And with you,

I'm done.

The Aftermath

After the memories of blushes,
The wishes of kisses,
The, 'I miss you's,' and 'I love you's,'

The unstoppable heartbeats.

The late night texting,
The long hours calling,
The midnight drive –
Staring into the other's eyes.

The moments you slept in bed together,
Legs wrapped,
Cradled in your lover's arm.

You both felt this was the time,
That this was the moment,
Perfect and right.

And you experience something,
Together,
For the first time.

You made your privates, public,
As a train into a tunnel,
They intertwined.

– Then what?

When these once unforgettable memories
Become the things you want to forget,
the things that haunt you
And leave some sense of regret?

– What then?

When these blushes turn into heated rushes,
And all you want,
Is them out of your face.

When these kisses,
turn into disses,
about how smelly their breath was.

When the, 'I miss you's,' and 'I love you's,'
Turn into,
"I hate you, leave me alone."

When your heart no longer skips a beat for them,
You stop texting, calling, driving with them.

No more staring into the other's eyes,
You've both become something you despise.

When your privates, remain private and they no longer
intertwine.

– Then what?

With the emotions and confusion,
maintaining your daily lives,

Which at one point included the both of you.

Engaging in society,
You are bound to meet again.

Once loved,
Their name engraved on your brain.

Moving on is the only way.
Yet, it is not as easy,
as it is to say.

– What then?

When your once partner has moved on
And all you have are the memories of was,

What then is there to be done,
Coping with the aftermath of love?

Walk Out

It seems that I've gotten attached to you,
Now you don't want me around.
I'm sorry I considered you a friend,
I'm sorry for myself again.

I always seem to let people in,
Give too much trust –
The benefit of the doubt,
Then they toss me out.

I honestly thought this wouldn't happen,
It seems I'm the one who's the fool.
Silly of me, to think you'd stick around,
At least to grab some food.

I don't think I would really blame you,
Like me,
You have trust issues.
I know it can hurt to let people in,
But remember,
It can hurt to lose them too.

Now I have to start all over again.
How many times has it been?
Will I ever forgive?

I'm only trying to make sense of this.
Most of my life has been a blank disk.

I guess it's best,
That I face this by myself.

Then along comes another person,
Barging into my life.

I have grown to hate,
Greetings, accompanied with smiley faces,
Of great Intentions,
Inviting me out to different places.

When the truth is,
You walk in,
To walk right out.

In the end, I have come to learn –
This is simply how life goes.

When It Hurts

It was 10 a.m.

And those hurtful words dug deep into my bones,
They cut my flesh.

I cried my eyes till they were bloodshot red,
I bit my lip, withholding what I feared to release the most.

I wanted to scream for help –
Scream for love.
I tried to call down hope from above.

I needed something to ease my pain.

It was 10 a.m.

I made way to meet a friend,
On a public bus – wedged between two men.

I knew they saw my weary eyes,
Heard my sniffles –
The anger that rose from the inside!

The mixed emotions that contained a sad story.

It was 10 a.m.

I sat on a bench – It was silent.

At that point,
I had shut my surroundings out,
At that point –
Black tee, pants, and shoes,
Is where depression came about.

Familiar faces appeared as foes.
Distraught,
I couldn't trust anymore.

To passing strangers,
I'd put on a smile.
If they stopped and asked,
I'd tell them, "I'm fine."

Though I knew,
Deep within,
I was no longer alive.

Demons crept in, spoon fed me their lies,
That I was not of worth,
That I am meant to die.

I thought about my life,
And how much I've deprived myself of the care and love I
deserve.

I am not a disappointment.
And maybe, one day,
I'll believe.

I Am Not

Don't you ever dare say,
For one moment,
I walked away.

– You pushed me to the edge.
You didn't want me near.

I wanted to be there.
I tried to show I cared.

But, It's your lack of trust,
That put a dent in us.

So don't you blame me –
I'm not the wolf of this tale.

Lack Of Ability

I question my level of stability.
Being able to stand,
Devastating thoughts,
Great memories long gone –
I wish I could have savored.

I sense the fault of my falls.
My self sabotaging ways –
Corrupted truth,
I so easily believed in.

Never being able to cross the line,
Nor where I draw the line to be crossed.

I have drowned myself:
The pursuit of love.

Refusal of vulnerability –
I don't open.
Without doubt:
It leaves me broken.

I have learnt,
The past dictates my present choices.

Failed Effort

I tried my best,
To impress your heart.

Expressing till I stress,
But you put me off.

Like garbage in the bin,
You tossed me to the wind.

Now here I lay,
Whimpering softly.

Recognize

Recognize;

What we once had,
And what we once were,
And where we saw ourselves,
In time to come,
Was nothing,

But a flawed dream of ours.

Betrayal

With you I shared my hope,

Now around my throat,

You have a rope.

Mislead

The itsy and the bitsy,
Of your web
Coerced the trachea of my being.

Strum the string of my voice,
As the bow to a violin instructs the tune –
Off key,
It screeches the things it never means.

Deprived of oxygen:
My intestines refluxed.

I digest every bit,
Before the chance to chew.

Little did they know,
I was never to be.

The musical notes,
You have longed to erased,
Presenting a harmonious symphony.

A true image,
An accurate reflection,
Of a once distorted plea.

I will do whatever I must,
To sing,
What song is left of me.

Devil's Advocate

I remember the nights,
the devil laid beside me in bed.
How he'd love and torture me,
Between the covers.
Behind the closed doors,
It was a different story.

We seemed perfect together,
Match made in heaven.
Fallen from glory –
We were not perfect.
My claws and his torches,
At each other's necks.

We had long knew;
By the cross roads,
This wouldn't work,
Yet, we scratched the match and lit the candle
Anyways.

How I settled for less with him,
How I told myself I knew my worth,
And didn't change a damn thing.

I damned myself to this hell,
When I had the chance and didn't leave.
Feeding myself lies –
He'll come around and change.

God never made me the Devil's Advocate.
I loved you,
Till I was worn out.
Yet, you never loved me the same.

Then finally I mustered the strength to flee.

I remember the nights,
The devil laid beside me in bed.
How he'd love and torture me,
Between the covers.
Behind the closed doors,
It was a different story.

I awoke to what was all a dream.
Not the part about the devil,
But the part where I actually leave.

Fireworks

I saw fireworks last night–
It made me think of you,
And what we could have been,
If you stayed.

Adulthood

"And the child grew and became strong."

A Day in June

Remember the sun always shines after the rain,
And that a rabbit comes out of its hole,
When it feels safe.
I'll be under the mango tree,
Eating a few of the mangoes I see.
Whenever you feel free,
Feel free to visit me.
Then we can sit back and chill,
Just like children.
Thinking about the times,
The real world,
Was never real to you or I.

Deep Thoughts

I lay in the bed with deep thoughts.
My mind speaks the loudest.
It analyzes the life it has lived.

The memories captured:
The good and the bad ones.

I lay in the bed with deep thoughts.
Deep questions, Deep Hurts, Deep loss.

A moment of passion,
I exist, Then I'm gone.

I lay in the bed with deep thoughts,
Which keeps me restless a lot.

So, whenever It becomes too much,
I prove myself weak,
And I let a tear fall.

Run

Momma said "run,"
I remember being young.
This world, A safe haven,
I've learnt, is broken.

Playgrounds for children,
Later became battlefields for adults.
We will all one day grow up:
I wish I truly knew this.

When Momma said "run,"
Her arms stretched beyond my needs,
Healed the bruises that bleed.

This world has taught another soul,
That there are arms out there:
Harsh and cold –
And Momma,
That your arms won't always be there.

Yet, when Momma said "run,"
The world around me never mattered –
And many times,
Do I, again wish, it never did.

I am different

I've been told mean things.
I've been looked down upon.
I barely equal to what society calls,
'Good enough'.
And that's okay,
I'm fine with that:
'If I am not better, At least I am different.'

– Jean-jacques Rousseau (1712 -1778)

Something Good

Cheers to –

The strangers who became friends.
The childless couple who became parents.
The elderly grandpa with amazing stories.
The girl or boy who stood up for themselves.
The guy out of prison with a whole new mindset.
The girl in foster care who finally got adopted.

In this cycle of life,
Through the ups and downs,
There is always something good in the making.

Faded Hope

What will I be when I grow up?

What will I do?

Will I have a cool job?

Well,
I'm grown now.

– And how childish it was of me to ask those questions.

Late Nights

Late Night drives,
To ease the mind.
Forgive me,
If I shed a few tears.
I am,
But bone and flesh.
I need rest:
It is hard to find.
Three hours have passed –
It didn't feel like that.
By now,
My v-neck is drenched.
Life to me,
Has not been the best.
Freedom,
Has only known me in the night.
The night accepts me for me.
I love my late night drives –

When I'm behind the wheel.

At Least

When I say that,
"At least I'm alive,"
What I mean is:
I am a mess.

I once held a knife at my throat,
To cut in half my final breath.

I aimed a gun at my forehead,
A fully loaded pistol:
My finger under pressure.

I tipped my weight,
On a seven story building,
Hoping that gravity would do the rest.

When I say that,
"At least I'm alive,"
What I mean is:
I have fought a fight to be here.

Playing a game I could never win,
The devil carves 'death' on my chest.
Longing to die -
I'm unhappy with myself.

In childhood memories,
I scream for help.

I hear my cries,
That would not end.

When I say
"At least I'm alive,"
What I mean is:
My funeral isn't written in stone.

God has a plan –
That I know nothing of.

And though I may still have a lot to overcome,
I can say that,
"At least I'm alive."

Work

"By the sweat of your brow you will eat your bread."

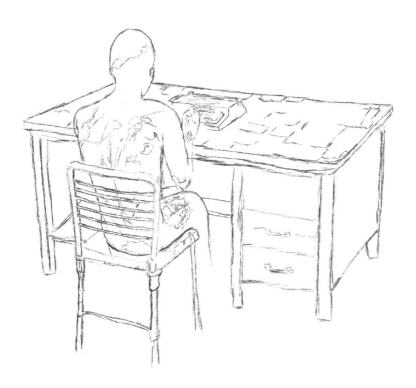

Prostitution

I am fathomed,
I do not understand;
Why it is we choose to ridicule those who prostitute,
To sell their bodies –

As if we have never sold our bodies too.

As though they don't have bills to pay,
And mouths to feed.
A college tuition fee that's long overdue.

Brother's bail is set at $10,000,
Only five more nights of work are required to set him free.

Not all prostitutes work the streets,
They work 'modest' jobs,
In malls and law offices.

The light of day,
They have 'decent' jobs,
But decent jobs hardly ever
Make decent pay.

And we all know this.

Working 9-5;
Minimum wage,
Monthly expenses,

Exceeding profit,
Banking our lives for dollars –

As if we have never sold our bodies too.

Prostitution is the choice of those
Whose choices are few,
Their bodies become their last resort.

Their bodies gifted
To the hands of men,
In hopes that they will lift them up.

Or in hopes
That they can survive
Another day,
Trying to live life like anyone else.

Being prejudiced doesn't help. So,

I am fathomed,
I do not understand;
Why It is we choose to ridicule those who prostitute,
To sell their bodies –

As if we have never sold our bodies too.

No Pay

Unemployment –
You're a bastard.
How dare you,
Undermining;
The lack of education,
Prior experience –
My ass.
I didn't ask you,
I told you,
I needed to eat too.
Independence is only hard,
When robbed of opportunity.
And the Government
Talking shit,
About entrepreneurship
– Enrichment.
Easy for you to say,
When your life is a pedestal.
When youths choose violence
Over peace –
I don't blame them.
When minimum wage is lower
Than gas prices
How the hell, Do you expect people
To go on striving?
Unemployment –
You communist of a dictatorial nation,
Suffering its Citizens to be inferior.

Daydreaming

It is a living nightmare;
Gifting hours,
To mega companies –
Feeding on their pennies and dimes.

Mortified,
Men and women,
Shredded to bones –
Cremated in time.

Simply to create a future,
Merely that their children
Can stay alive.

It is hard to dream, a life, in
A world,
where survivability is but a lie.

Yet,
Daydreaming,
Realms where happiness exist,
It is the soul of what keeps us revived.

Less Than

I hear the whispers.
I hear the whispers of voices,
Chittering and chattering,
My name.
Incompetent of completing –
Her task and duties.
She is not fit,
This is a man's world.
A man's place,
Do not step in.

I am tired of being considered less than.

Food For Thought

During lunch breaks,
I eat my meal and fill my stomach to its content.
Consciously gorging every bit.
Never ensure to wipe my lips.
A peaceful place to contemplate,
On thoughts that have weighed heavy –
Shoulders grown weary.
How can I improve?
Where did I go wrong?
I bet my supervisor must be pissed.
There is so much to think about.

Yet, I eat my meal and fill my stomach to its content.

Interview

The email states:
Ensure the best of attire is worn.
Ladies,
That your shoes don't overstep your dress.
And males,
Please don't wear jeans and call it 'top tier'.
Hair, well groomed, is due.
Inclusive of both parties.
Perfume may be worn, but only in moderation.
We refuse to accept anything less than the best.

Any signs of nervousness will be noted.

So a word of advice,
Leave your anxiety at the door.
Your deep breaths – sighs of frustration at the door.

Any signs of nervousness will be noted.

Just behind the door you will find both the hiring manager and
department manager seated.
Give a smile upon entrance.
Give your absolute best.

Don't have to take my word for it –
You know you're in need of employment.
I think your savings accounts may speak for themselves,
Your unpaid bills may speak for themselves.

The growl of your stomach,
Or the drive to be independent.

Any signs of nervousness will be noted.

Will you forfeit your chance before it is even received?
Stammers and stutters are unacceptable.
Straight forward answers permitted only.
If you stray from the topic at hand, You will be addressed.

Any signs of nervousness will be noted.

Your pain will soon come to an end.
Answer the questions, truthfully as you can.
Ensure eye contact is maintained.

Thank both the hiring manager, department manager,
individually, for their time.
Reward their kindness towards you with a warm smile.

Leave through the doors which you came.
You may gather the deep breaths and sighs of frustration you left
there.
You are free to go.
In the days preceding, A call will be made to the contact number
in which you have provided.
Your interview session is complete.

Dear Manager

Dear Manager,

To all the days I clocked in late, or called sick – It was intentional.

Sincerely,

Your employee.

P.S – Tell HR, I'on care, lololl!

Home

"By wisdom a house is built, and by understanding it is established."

Transparent Source

(To all the rainy days.)

Beautiful oasis,
Droplet traces, in places unreachable.
When rain reigns life –
It rejuvenates.
A sprout of hope.
All humanity;
Water separates,
And joins.
The sea of forever.
A cup of momentary.
Embrace the transparent source.

Thanks

(To my bed with love.)

Thanks for being my safe space, my shoulder to lean on– the secrets you and I share will never fade.

Freedom

(To our ancestors who survived.)

Eska told me everything would be okay.
I remember the look in her eyes, glistening with tears.
She was always hopeful, even in the worst of situations.
Her skin from God; the soil of the earth, emphasized our
resilience as black people. She was never afraid of what the
world around us had to say.
The curls that made her crown, she often let fall down, never
discarding their royalty.
Dark, luscious, and saturated with moisture: she appreciated
them.
She told me to appreciate my curls too, to always appreciate how
Abba father made me.
Her physique, small built, was nothing. She had a spirit animal;
meek as a sheep, with the powerful rush of a lion. She was
fierce.
Locking hands, we ran as can, across the cane estate to freedom.
Eska told me everything would be okay.

We didn't make it far— But I still believed her.

Peace

I hear C's on the piano,
In the background playing.
I hear the waves echoing –
They solemnly reverberate.
Wind chiming,
As whispering children's voices.

I know I have found my place.

Free Life

Now I lay me down to sleep –
It is 10 p.m.

My arms and knees curled across the pillow –
By 11.

Refusing to let go,
I clench tighter by 12.

I cannot sleep.

My eyes teared open –
I stare at the ceiling.

This is mine.

This is freedom.

Independence at its peak.

Without much thought,
I rip the covers from above.
Jumping on the bed,
Bought with my own money.

Strolling to the kitchen,
At 1 a.m.
I brew some coffee,
While I try to call a friend.

It is 2 a.m.

I am capable of doing this all on my own.
The moment I have long awaited since my teens.
A place to call my home,
Where I dictate the rules.

I glance at the ceiling and smile.

This is mine.

This is freedom.

Independence at its peak.

It is 3 a.m.
I can finally sleep.

Like You

Dad just left like that.
He's always running.
I don't know this man.
Supposedly,
I'm the spitting image of him –
I refuse to run though.
Sometimes, I wish I got to know him,
But maybe it's all for the best.
Would have probably been more hurt than dignified.
Grandfather wasn't any different.
Dad became the man he saw hitting his mother.
I hit myself sometimes.
Still, I don't understand life,
But if I ever have a Child,
They'll never feel how I had.

Sex

"May you always be captivated by her love."

Feel Good

It felt good for the moment –

I won't lie.

But,

A moment isn't good enough to satisfy.

Foreplay

Chills beneath the warm touch –
Your fingers:
A paint brush.

My skin:
A canvas of expression.

Explosion of rainbows.
Streams of rivers.

This canal,
An entrance to a world of peace.

You have found your abode within me.

Head First

Swollen eyes of tears,
I uttered,
"I am afraid, I have never done this before."

Adulthood comes with more than just pain,
There is also pleasure.

Amongst my silent sobs,
I ask you to go easy.

You chuckled and responded,
"Easy is my middle name."

Some days,
I do hate you.

Yet,
With your head devoured between my thighs,
I closed my eyes –
And chose to love you.

Loving Creation

I taste the lust on your lips as they caress mine.

The butter balm bliss –
The longing you've been waiting for.

We've been waiting for,
This God given moment to getaway.

Hidden in the bushes as Adam and Eve –
The garden of Eden.

Unashamed to exhibit our nakedness before one another.

You were mine way before your mother's conception.

You were designed for me,
And I made in the image of you.

We are the missing pieces to our beautiful puzzles.

And I delight in the nights,
When you make us feel whole.

Too Good

I want a love that's too good to be true.
90 Degree showers.
Breast pressed,
Nipples pop.
A table set for two.
Make-up sex in the dining room.
Waited so long,
My patience stretched for you.

A figment of my dreams;
I count the hours as they tick by,
Tick the calendar as the days fly.
I'll find you.
As far as the heaven's above,
My guardian angel,
You give life.

Talk to me in the dark of the night,
Remind me what love feels like.
I'm hoping for you,
You're hoping for me –
To walk away doesn't feel right.

Dance with me in this moonlight,
I see sparks in our cocoon tonight.
So darling,
Please hurry,
Our time is more than precious –
Emotions too strong to let them die.

Desires

These desires won't go.

I want someone to hold.

Comfort me,

Remind me,

I am not alone.

Woman

Let me touch the roaring waters.
Let me touch on what makes you a woman.
Let's explore,
This body –
This temple,
Given to us by the God of this world.
Let us go,
To where,
The wildest of dreams can roam.

Let us,
Call there,
Home.

Eiffel Tower

Eiffel tower legs,
Made crooked.

Side to side,
The neck –
A deadlock.

Empire state building;
Falls,
Plows,
Below,
The ground.

Broken sprinklers,
Saturate the base.

The two structures,
Touch.

Screeching names –
They can not bear it.

Praying God,
Have mercy.

Flipping seats,
At dinner tables;
The guest,
Becomes the meal.

Take hold the knife and fork,
Consume this very being.

These Eiffel tower legs,
Satisfy,
Empire state building needs.

Time

"For there is a time - there for every purpose and for every work."

The Clock

The clock reminds me of the time.

The time present,
The time foregone,
And set before me.

They say count your blessings,
So I count the hours allotted.

I pick the flower petals,
And tossed them;
For the souls I have met,
The love I have Received,
Given, and Lost.

The clock reminds me of the time.

The days when I could close my eyes and take life by the hand –
Holding on to dear life.
When muscles and bones do not play a tune, every time I attempt
to move.
Where meals were not portioned,
And the pressure within my veins did not entrap me.

The clock reminds me of the time.

The days where I was free and time was not a factor.
The seconds spent at the seashore,

Made me feel sure,
That this life would go on forever.
Friends beholding my presence after a long summer break –
Filled with laughter and girl power,
No one could separate.

The clock reminds me of the time,
How my time is almost finished now.

It is five past the midnight hour,
And I am still here.
I cannot explain this phenomenon,
However,
I will cherish every moment of it.

Choices

Why are you upset with me?
You're the one who settled down.

That was your fairy tale,
I didn't want that.

I didn't want a man,
What I needed was money.

Stability;
I achieved, The longing –
On my own.

Desiring financial freedom;
I needed to build myself,
I needed to build my dreams.

My God!
I desire,
My poetry to be known.

Out there in the streets,
As one of the greatest
Poets of all time.

Flying with the eagles;
Maya Angelou,
Shakespeare,
King David.

Rest in peace,
Hands down,
Engraved on my tombstone.

Don't get mad at me for putting myself first –
My life on hold,
That was my choice.

At the end of the day;
You wrote your story,
You made your bed,
Now hold your own.

Beautiful

Dripping in melanin –
Beautiful, she was.
Eyes, Alluring for miles.
Smiles brought feelings alive.
Why at five?
When our shoelaces we couldn't tie.

Dripping in melanin –
Beautiful, she was.
I longed for her.
Yet silent, on the matter,
I remained.
Pressing to impress –
The secret lover was I.

Dripping in melanin –
Beautiful, she was.
This truth,
In fact, Was no lie.
This truth,
In fact, At times,
I denied.

Beautiful, She was.
Yet,
Never did I make her mine.

In Time

It is said,
That nothing ages better than fine wine.
Crimson red, sweet and divine –
Just like God made you.

Eyes cannot lie,
Seeing you develop –
Refined over time,
It's proof that God is faithful.

They say that a woman is her best, In a dress.
Christian Dior ball gown,
Louis Vuitton handbags,
Jimmy Choo stilettos –
Though exceptionally elegant,
They will all one day fade,
But you will always remain.

How you –
Walk through the door and grace the aisles.
How you smile when you are greeted.
Full steam ahead,
You go beyond what's expected –
Accepting the challenge,
Even to the end.

No words of gratitude could ever repay.
Neither silver,

Neither Gold,
Nor rubies compensate.
A genuine heart is rare.

In fifty years,
Many will know you by name.
A legacy held firm will not pass away –
Your efforts paved this pathway.

From humble beginnings,
To now appreciated –
Good things will always come to those who wait.

Acceptance

"Marvelous are thy works."

Confession

I confess,
I have not always been the best person.
How over time the monsters in my life
Finally consumed me.
How I allowed Jesus to so much erase my past;
I had almost forgotten me,
And who I was,
Or who I felt at times, I still am.
As a child with smoke in their hand,
And no one stopped them.
Anxiety rattled bones,
Depression hurtling towards the floor.
They'll say,
You have no reason,
When you have Jesus to make you smile.
Read the word of God and be cured:
Even after I've repeated the psalms a thousand times.
I still feel the damage,
The scars on my abdomen of a once escapee.
Traumatized,
Of the things I've done.
In hopes, I'll find solace,
And forgive myself of them all.

Upper Hand

I have come to learn the mismanagement of men.

Fingers wrapped around the throat,
Gasping for your very breath.

The comforting fabric of a bed,
Ragingly ripped from beneath.

Pinned against a flesh grating wall,
Sweat dripping – as the temple bleeds.

"Give me my Baby!"
He swifts away –
Your precious gift from God.

Hearing screams of an infant,
Is a terrorizing sound.

How a broken teen watches, A family broken down.

Etched the hurt that would last,
Seeing trauma as the stain –
As dashing Fire onto a flame.

"Let her go!"
Heat of boiling blood,
Constricting in my veins.

A sharp knife pointed:
Authority masquerade.
Nervousness of shaking hands –
Gave it all away.

Yanking, One more,
Dad makes it out the Door.
Swift away with baby –
She cries for mother's warmth.

Mom runs to save her child.
My Heart rate – on incline.

I am later told,
It was not abuse,
So don't you dare tell a lie.

Pleasure

I know what pleasure feels like.
The truth is I'm terrified.
I could say I don't deserve,
But it's more than that.
It reminds me of times I fear,
So I fight myself,
Day– Night.
Physically– Pound, Mentally– Drown, Spiritually– Decay.
Ridding myself of something God naturally gave.
I have seen the ladies in porn,
Seeing what they enjoy,
Yet, never at all enjoying the same.
Hated the ladies screaming between thrust,
Always felt it was weak, and quite derogative.
Giving a man so much power to wield:
Every in and exhale.
I denied myself.
Lied to myself.
Did I ever wonder what it was like –
For once,
To be choked by a man,
To be lust and love at the same time.
No, I refused.
Shamed myself till I believed,
That my body –
Unworthy of such gain.

Mirror Mirror

Soft touches turn brutal
In the face of cruelty.
When grooming becomes first hand,
The lessons taught remain.
Carving into a mini version of them;
Into a person you never thought of being,
Their actions curtailing your every move.
Little children no longer run from him –
They run away from you.
The mirror shows how much twin you both are.
A wrecked, tarnished being;
You're both empty,
And now seek to draw the innocence of everyone else.

Reminder

Why do lost souls
find themselves;
Where water cascades,
Turquoise parades –
Limitless seas.
I guess it screams,
Freedom.
It screams,
Home.
A place where birds don't mind eating,
The same fishes we eat of.
Where rejection isn't found,
Nations abound,
Refuge to the hated.
Or perhaps,
We hope for a little too much.
Why do the seas find themselves
Where lost souls
Come to gaze?

–Well, we all need a reminder of our existence.

Verbal Haunt

The role of the eldest sibling is hard.
Witness to all hidden in the home,
Before the public eyes intrude.
Often compelled –
Act as though all is made well.

Becoming the shield,
While The parents wield,
Uncontrollably, their despair.
Solemnly, whispers –
The elder to the younger
"Everything will be okay,"

Until, Screaming Adults,
Raise hell in the background.

It dawns at night –
Weighs heavy,
When innocent eyes are burnt –
And deprived of a childhood they deserve.

How the memories have haunt,
Now that you're an adult,
Yet, you still have to keep moving on.

Accepting Reality

There's nothing here.
No remains in the ashtray;
The toddler from yesterday,
accidentally spilt it all.
Don't look forward to a
Thank you letter in the mail.
There's limited space,
Plus, you don't fit the criteria.
Just start fresh.
Forget the past,
Where you foolishly
placed others ahead of you.
Where pain is but a backfilled valley.
Wipe tears –
Forgiveness written on your forehead.
Weary of the nice at heart,
Nothing sustainable to hold on.
Mist of smoke fading.
There is nothing here.
The ash in the ashtray
was only taking up space –
The toddler spilt it yesterday.
And simply, like breathing,
I used a broom and swept it away.

Loss

She's kind of just going through a lot,
I mean she's been through a lot:
She had to accept that there would be no apology.
No thank you letter,
No forgiveness.
She hides in the closet,
And talks to herself.
She's kind of lost it.
Self pity,
Or release,
You know, Whatever these millennials call it.
She's kind of shock at the person she was,
So much she finds it hard to breathe.
She's just remembering,
How much of a monster she is,
That truly, memoirs exist because of these.
A freak, A gay, A predator –
The realization that in the eyes of the world,
She will never be anything,
But A sob on bended knees.

Inadequacy

I have felt inadequate.
I have looked many times in the mirror and wish the body that I
lived in was never mine.
I wished long ago I gave it up like the Holy Ghost, holy – divine.
I must confess, I have looked at my parents with despair – hate
built within me.
Wishing I was never born or wishing they failed to conceive –
me.
I have looked many times towards my siblings,
Broken hearted.
Wishing the hand of time to rewind,
That I could have been the better sibling;
Wishing I were the parent,
Wishing I could have given them the life that they deserved.
In all honesty;
I have hoped for many things,
Have said many things,
Felt many things,
If only circumstances were different.

Sad

If only I could reverse time,
Maybe then my life wouldn't be as sad.

Closure

"The truth sets you free."

Young

Do you remember when we were young,

And we could run,

And frolic free in the summer?

A shoulder

She was afraid –
Alone.
All she ever wanted was love.
Not a lover.
Rather a shoulder to lean on.

Gone

I am left with nothing but the shambles.

The shingles itching my elbows and knees.

The paranoia,

That something is watching.

Lights flickering – a deer in headlights.

A young child's hand leads me:

Called me grand.

I am sorry for the life,

That has left an aging body.

Hopefully, it appreciated the memories.

Squinting lids,

And crows feet,

Binocular lens to see.

I attend funerals,

That the bereaved,

May attend mines too.

I hang in the morgue of a funeral home,

I behold the body of a once god;

Aged,

Withered

And cold,

But not forgotten.

Deceiving

I'm not a good person.
I'm misleading.
I'm a liar –
To myself and others.
I know what I want to be,
And won't be it.
I know where I want to go,
And won't go.
I know that I'm lost,
And insist that I'm not.
I'm a storm of rain clouds,
Cunning others to believe,
I'm a blossom of flowers.
I'm a bundle of stagnant mess,
Speculations arising between breaths.
There's a rope hanging from the tree,
And I accept the guilty plea.
Swinging from the limb,
There is no good left in me.

Masquerade

I have learned,
Even the devil masquerades as an angel of light,
So take heed that not everyone is as they seem.

Death

"Life and Death is in the Power of the Tongue: Choose life."

Fumes

Exhales of hell on earth.

Living corpse,

With coffins as living quarters.

Revolutionary suicide:

Cigarettes –

The convenient grenade.

Bombs inside the chest.

Coals for lungs: burning –

Dancing in the fumes of death.

Ashes to Ashes,

Dust to Dust –

Your end is coming.

It's here.

Disintegrating

Disintegrating bodies –
This body.
A temple of ruins –
The remains.
A skeleton of use to;
I use to,
And now I don't.
A sanctuary of praise.
God,
I know you hear me,
Leave me not on deaf ears.
Restore this body –
This disintegrating body.
And withholding nothing,
Make new:
My damaged vessel.

Holy

God,
I pray you rip this soul,
From this dismay.
Shine your countenance upon my face.
Wipe away my sins;
Cast them into the sea of forget,
Or quench them in unbearable heat.
Take me to the land of milk and honey,
I've toiled this earth for too long.
I have seen the depths of the brutal,
And the demonizing of the innocent.
Laugh in the devil's face for me, why won't ya?
When the cherubim
Bring me to your celestial being.
And I will bow before you,
As the Jericho wall fell to its knees.

Maneuver

I watch the man,
Once a lion,
Become a Meerkat.
His limbs becoming limp,
Overtime.
His coat wear and tear –
The many battles it has fought,
Without rest.
He shakes his hand.
I assume that he is greeting me.
Yet, his eyes say otherwise.
Bittersweet good-byes.

I watched the man –
Once a yacht,
Demoted to a fishing boat.
Water dripping from the sides,
Unsteady balance, it capsizes.
Shriveled sticks,
Fail to hold the captain,
On and off shore.
The ship is slowly sinking,
He sheds a tear and smiles.

I watched the man,
Once the sun,
Transition to the moon.
A mere reflection,
Of what it was –
A memory from long ago.

Rotating around,
As the time flashes.

However aged,
It still shines.

The ghost of a hollow being,
Can not maneuver the host body.
Not like before,
Not like he used to.

I listen to the wails,
Of a once young man,
Creeping to the end of its road.

Solemnly Die

That one day flies so quickly,
Similar to the rain drops,
Splattered on windshields.

When rest is a hard ruby to attain,
Even after a full night,
Digging around for bed covers.

It is almost as though,
The stretched arms of man,
Could count the stars –
In just a few hours of freedom.

Stuffing, a vast galaxy inside a home.
The pavilions of poorly constructed four corners explode.

Really –
It was all money spent,
From something barely enjoyed –
Or seen.

Quiet vibrations ricocheting
within the space.
A corporate society named as the overlord.

A place of unforgiving smiles;
Always near Death,
The first taste of an internally worn out soul.

Days off,
Are the sounds of guns.
The clouds, echoing to you – run.

Remember the stars.
The gift of freedom.
The Universe way of –
Take a deep breath.

Even God had his day to rest.

Corporations slithering,
As sneaky snakes.
They have a way to keep
you a little longer.

We have a lot to restore ourselves.
We have given a lot of ourselves.

Die we all must,
As those behind us have,
Yet, don't die as everyone else had.

Sweet Revenge

You already told me,
My time would come.
That vengeance is way sweeter than the first act.

That death comes as a whisper,
Not a shout.
And all the evil that ever were,
Could never run.
I smile in the face of victory,
Or defeat,
Whichever suits my fancy.

I hope my enemies no longer doubt me.
I have fought the finishing fight.
Clouds of dust,
Surround about.
With my last drop of blood,
And smirk-ish smile,

I bravely relinquished my rights.

Unfortunate

Funerals are very few to me,
Am I fortunate to call it a blessing?

My apologies to all the real ones,
Who deserved that second chance,
And never received.

They begged God:
He didn't seem to hear –
Cried tears into the glass they drank from.

Every year,
Burying their existence,
That those on earth won't have to bear.

Unfortunately,
I don't know,
The weight you all must carry,
Until the day I have to carry my own.

— Remnant

Reference

Cover Page:
Le Negre Marron, 1967, Albert Mangones, Port-au-Prince, Haiti.

Birth:
NHS WindRush Nurses, 2021, Jak Buela, Whittington Hospital, London, UK.

Adolescence:
Moments Contained, 2022, Thomas J. Prince, Rotterdam, Netherlands.

Friendship:
Boonji Spaceman, 2021, Brendan Murphy, Hodges bay resort and spa, St.John, Antigua.

Love:
Redemption Song, 2003, Laura Facey, Emancipation Park, Kingston, Jamaica.

Heartbreak:
Awakening, 2019, Basil Watson, Miami, Florida, U.S.A.

Adulthood:
Ocean Atlas, 2014, Jason Decaires Taylor, Nassau, Bahamas.

Work:

The Lost Correspondent, 2006, Jason Decaires Taylor, The Lime, Grenada.

Home:
V.C Bird Monument, 2002, Andreas Gonzalez, St.John, Antigua.

Sex:
Awakening, 2019, Basil Watson, Miami, Florida, U.S.A.

Time:
Grand Jete, 1981, Enzo Plazzotta, Crane resort and residence, St.Philip, Barbados.

Acceptance:
Mama and Chi Dushi Culture, 2022, Hortence Brouwn, St.Anna Bay, Curacao.

Closure:
Windrush Generation Monument, 2022, Basil Watson, Waterloo Station, London, U.K.

Death:
Mahatma Gandhi, 1969, Forbes Burnham, Georgetown, Guyana.

Authors Note

Greetings Everyone, Get to know me!
My name is Kaiana. Generally, I'm really
reserved, and tend to be on the quiet side, however,
I am able to compensate via writing.
Here in your hands, you have a collection of my thoughts,
Curated with time and dedication.
I do hope they serve you well.

If you enjoy my work,
Follow me on Instagram.

Kaiana Cannonier

I'll see you there!